MARVELOUS
BODY

SEE INSIDE BODIES · WITH A MAGIC LENS

By **Jane Wilsher**

Illustrated by **Andrés Lozano**

Consultant: **Dr Kristina Routh,**
MBChB, MPH

What on Earth Books

What on Earth Books is an imprint of What on Earth Publishing
Allington Castle, Maidstone, Kent, ME16 0NB, United Kingdom
30 Ridge Road Unit B, Greenbelt, Maryland, 20770, United States

First published in the United States in 2022

Staff for this book: Publisher, Nancy Feresten; Editor, Patrick Skipworth;
Art Director, Andy Forshaw; Designer, Andy Mansfield

Book production and print production by Booklabs.co.uk

Consultant: Dr. Kristina Routh, MBChB, MPH

With thanks to Inclusive Minds for connecting us with their Inclusion Ambassador
network, in particular Jo Ross-Barrett for their input.

Library of Congress Cataloging-in-Publication Data available upon request

ISBN: 978-1-9137505-8-9

DC/Foshan, China/01/2022

Printed in China

10 9 8 7 6 5 4 3 2 1

whatonearthbooks.com

WHAT'S INSIDE

HOW TO USE THE MAGIC LENS

This book comes complete with an incredible invention—a magic lens that reveals the inner workings of the human body!

Just wave the magic lens over the page wherever you see a red pattern. Why not try it on the picture below?

Can you see the broken bone inside the cast?

 When you see the magic lens icon, use your lens to look at the red, patterned parts of the page to discover what's inside the body.

 When you see a picture of an eye, try to find all the body parts listed.

24-HOUR BODY

What can the body do, day in and day out?

So much. The human body is a fine-tuned machine. Different parts of the body work with each other, nonstop, 24-hours a day.

The body eats and drinks for energy. It learns and daydreams, too. Then it sleeps. The body grows and keeps on changing.

Remember, not all bodies work in the same way. Some people are able-bodied. Some are disabled. Some have medical conditions. Everyone is different.

LOOK INSIDE

Find out what the body can do every 24-hours.

the body...
makes the same amount of energy as about 25 lightbulbs—switched on.

the stomach muscles...
mix and churn up food, just like a blender.

the skin...
sheds up to 30,000 flakes of old skin.

hair...
grows about half a millimetre.

the chest...
moves up and down 20,000 times as you breathe air in and out of your lungs.

the brain...
thinks about 50,000 thoughts.

the mouth...
makes enough gloopy spit, or saliva, to fill two small empty juice cartons.

the heart...
beats about 100,000 times.

the ears...
listen to thousands of chitter-chatter words and sounds near and far away.

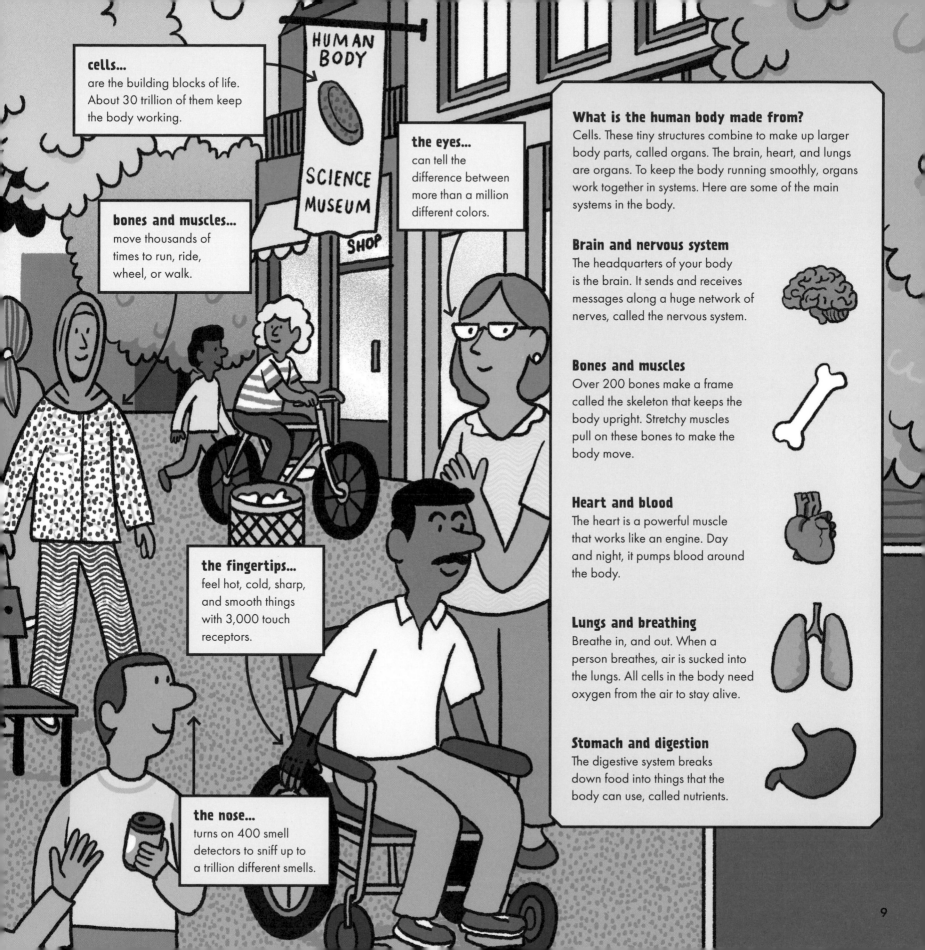

cells...
are the building blocks of life. About 30 trillion of them keep the body working.

bones and muscles...
move thousands of times to run, ride, wheel, or walk.

HUMAN BODY

SCIENCE MUSEUM

SHOP

the eyes...
can tell the difference between more than a million different colors.

the fingertips...
feel hot, cold, sharp, and smooth things with 3,000 touch receptors.

the nose...
turns on 400 smell detectors to sniff up to a trillion different smells.

What is the human body made from?
Cells. These tiny structures combine to make up larger body parts, called organs. The brain, heart, and lungs are organs. To keep the body running smoothly, organs work together in systems. Here are some of the main systems in the body.

Brain and nervous system
The headquarters of your body is the brain. It sends and receives messages along a huge network of nerves, called the nervous system.

Bones and muscles
Over 200 bones make a frame called the skeleton that keeps the body upright. Stretchy muscles pull on these bones to make the body move.

Heart and blood
The heart is a powerful muscle that works like an engine. Day and night, it pumps blood around the body.

Lungs and breathing
Breathe in, and out. When a person breathes, air is sucked into the lungs. All cells in the body need oxygen from the air to stay alive.

Stomach and digestion
The digestive system breaks down food into things that the body can use, called nutrients.

BRAIN POWER

As you read this page in this book, what does your brain do?

To make sense of the words and pictures, your brain sends messages, loads and loads of messages. Cells, called neurons, talk with each other through connections, called synapses.

Think of your brain as a powerful message center. Day and night, it controls your thinking, feeling, movement, and memory by sending and receiving millions of messages. It's your body's HQ.

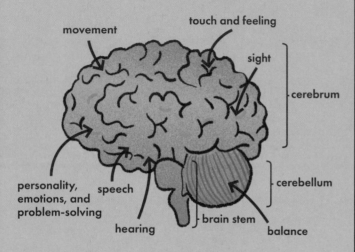

movement
touch and feeling
sight
cerebrum
personality, emotions, and problem-solving
speech
cerebellum
hearing
brain stem
balance

What do the different parts of the brain do?

This picture shows how different parts of the brain, called lobes, are connected with different jobs, or brain functions.

👁 **FIND IT** INSIDE AND OUTSIDE

You'll need the magic lens to find some of these things.

1. skull
2. neurons
3. synapses
4. pathway
5. brain stem
6. spinal cord
7. peripheral nerves
8. cerebrum
9. cerebellum
10. reflex action

LOOK INSIDE

Find out how your brain controls your body.

Inside the head

1 The **skull** is like a bony helmet that protects the delicate brain. Inside the skull, layers of tissue and a clear fluid keep the brain safe, like a cushion.

Making connections

2 The brain is made from billions of cells, called **neurons**. A microscope shows that neurons have tentacles or arms, which send and receive messages to and from other neurons.

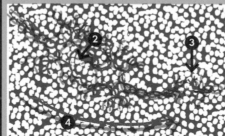

3 At the end of each tentacle, signals can pass from one neuron to the next. This space is called a **synapse**. Together, neurons, and synapses make a network across the body.

4 As you grow and learn, messages travel from one neuron to another, again and again, creating a **pathway**. The visual pathway helps you to read these words.

The nervous system

5 The **brain stem** keeps the heart, lungs, and digestive system working.

6 The brain stem is connected to a bundle of nerves called the **spinal cord**, which sends and receives messages around the body.

7 **Peripheral nerves** take and receive messages to and from the brain via the spinal cord.

If important nerves get damaged, they can leave a person unable to move parts of their body.

Reflexes

10 Sometimes the body does things without using the brain. This is called a **reflex action**. See what happens when you tap your leg just below your knee.

Memory and movement

8 When you remember something, many parts of the **cerebrum,** which is the top part of your brain, connect. Your short-term memory helps to remember things from seconds ago, your long-term memory from long ago.

9 At the back of the brain, the **cerebellum** controls movement and balance. Without it, the body would be unsteady and wobbly.

What do the five main senses do?

The senses help the body to keep in touch with the world by seeing, hearing, smelling, tasting, and touching. The senses also help to avoid danger.

Sight
Eyes can see a rainbow of colors, both near and far away.

Sound
Ears can hear a pin drop or loud crashing music.

Smell
A nose can smell a sweet flower or the warning smell of rotten food.

Taste
Smell and taste work together to show if something is good or bad to eat.

Touch
Touch is about feeling. Feel the softness of your face. Touch also warns of hot, dangerous things.

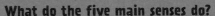

EYES

How many times a day do you blink?

Up to an amazing 30,000 times. Just think: your eyes are shut for over one hour each day. Blinking helps to keep the eyes clean.

Eyes can open wide to see the wonders of the world, both up close and far away. They take in vast amounts of information and light, which the brain turns into your view of the world.

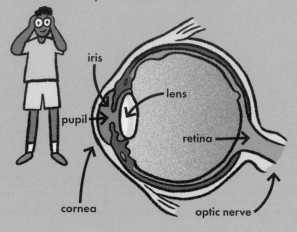

iris
lens
pupil
retina
cornea
optic nerve

How big are the eyes?

Bigger than you think. This picture shows one eye from the side. A gel-filled ball, called the eyeball, sits in a socket deep inside the head.

FIND IT INSIDE AND OUTSIDE

You'll need the magic lens to find some of these things.

1. eyebrow
2. eyelashes
3. eyelid
4. tear ducts
5. cornea
6. pupil
7. iris
8. lens
9. retina
10. optic nerve

LOOK INSIDE

Find out how the eyes help to see.

Parts of the eye

Different parts of the eye work together.

1. The **eyebrow** sits on the top of the bony socket that keeps the eyeball safe. Hair on the eyebrow stops sweat from running into the eye.

2. **Eyelashes** stop all kinds of grit and dirt from flying into the eyes.

3. The **eyelid** closes when we blink.

4. Salty water from the **tear ducts** keep the eyes wet and wash away any dirt.

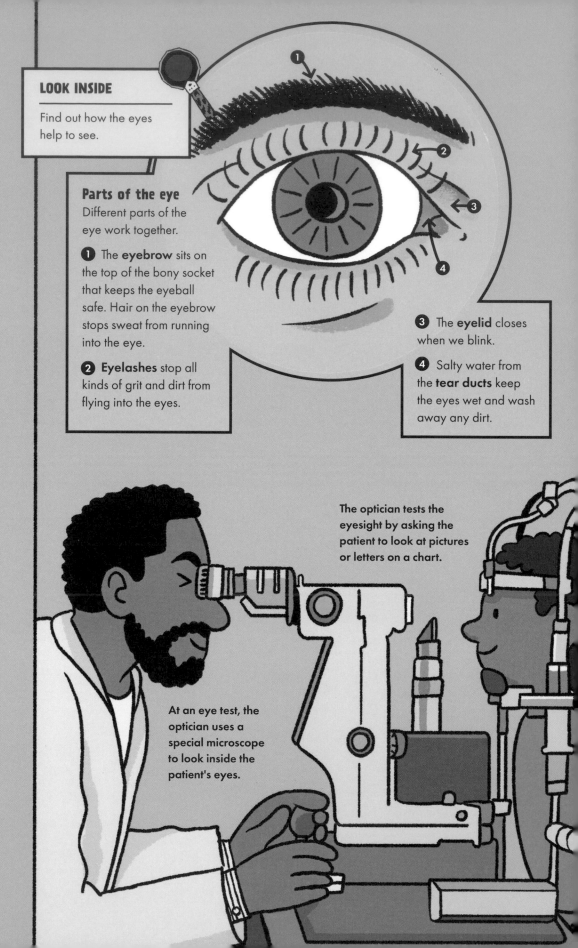

The optician tests the eyesight by asking the patient to look at pictures or letters on a chart.

At an eye test, the optician uses a special microscope to look inside the patient's eyes.

How do eyes see?

It's all about the journey of light travelling through the eye.

5 Light enters the eye through the **cornea**, which is a clear layer that bends and directs rays of light.

6 The black **pupil** is actually a hole that lets light into the eye.

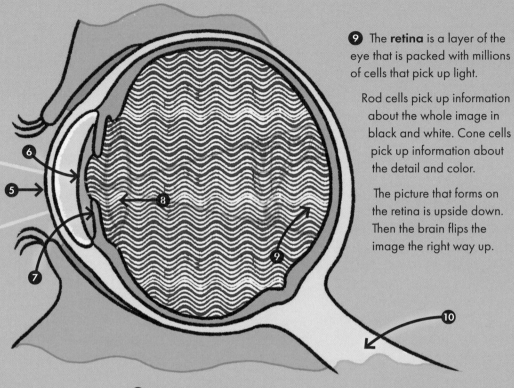

9 The **retina** is a layer of the eye that is packed with millions of cells that pick up light.

Rod cells pick up information about the whole image in black and white. Cone cells pick up information about the detail and color.

The picture that forms on the retina is upside down. Then the brain flips the image the right way up.

7 The **iris** is the colored part of the eye. It controls the size of the pupil to let in more or less light. The pupil is bigger in dim light and smaller in bright light.

8 The **lens** is a curved layer inside the eyeball that helps to direct light towards the retina.

10 Signals from the retina travel along the **optic nerve** to the brain.

Why do some people wear glasses?

Glasses can help a person to see more clearly. If you are nearsighted, you can see things nearby, but not far away. If you are farsighted, you can see things in the distance but not nearby.

Tinted glasses can protect us from bright lights, which can be painful or damaging to some people's eyes.

nearsighted

farsighted

EARS

Why are ears shaped like flexible cones?

The cone shape helps to collect invisible sound waves, or ripples of air. It gathers and directs the waves into the ear holes.

The sound waves travel through three parts of the ear, called the outer ear, the middle ear, and the inner ear. Then signals are sent to the brain. "CRASH! BANG!" The sounds are heard.

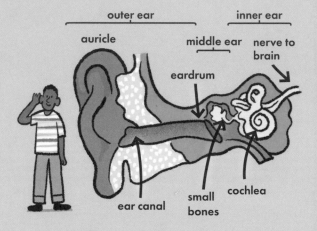

outer ear — inner ear

auricle — middle ear — nerve to brain

eardrum

cochlea

ear canal — small bones

What happens inside the ear?
This picture shows what the inside of the ear looks like from a side view.

👁 **FIND IT INSIDE AND OUTSIDE**
You'll need the magic lens to find some of these things.

❶ sound waves	❼ hammer
❷ auricle	❽ anvil
❸ ear hole	❾ stirrup
❹ ear canal	❿ cochlea
❺ wax	⓫ nerves
❻ eardrum	

❶ **Sound waves** are ripples of air, called vibrations. You can't see them, but ears pick up all kinds of sound waves, from the ping of a phone to the thumping beat of loud music.

Outer ear

❷ You can see some of the outer ear—the **auricle**—but the rest is hidden inside the head. Each auricle is shaped like a shell to collect sound waves.

❸ The auricle scoops the sound waves into the ear through the **ear hole**.

❹ The sound waves continue on through the **ear canal**.

❺ **Wax** in the ear canal helps to trap dirt and stop it from getting too far into the ear.

❻ When the sound waves hit the **eardrum**, it starts to vibrate. This means it wobbles really fast, just like the top of a drum.

Middle ear

In the middle ear, three small bones pick up the sound vibrations and pass them through the ear. These bones are the tiniest in the body.

7 **Hammer** bone

8 **Anvil** bone

9 **Stirrup** bone

Ear canal

These tiny bones work together, moving backward and forward to rattle the vibrations through the middle ear.

Inner ear

In the inner ear, the vibrations are turned into signals.

10 The **cochlea** is shaped like a snail. It is filled with liquid and tiny hairs that pick up the vibrations and convert them into signals.

11 These signals travel along **nerves** to the brain, which can tell the difference between a single musical note and loud cheering. The brain also works out where the sounds come from.

LOOK INSIDE

Follow the invisible journey of sounds and discover how ears pick them up.

NOSE AND TONGUE

Why can't you taste food when you have a cold?

Blame a stuffy nose! The nose and tongue work like a double act to pick up smells and tastes. If the nose can't smell, it's difficult to taste.

The nose and tongue are gatekeepers. They send signals to help the brain decide what it is safe to let into the body. They also pick up warnings of danger, such as the smell of burning.

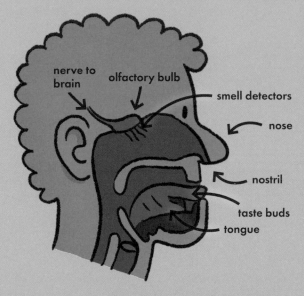

nerve to brain
olfactory bulb
smell detectors
nose
nostril
taste buds
tongue

How are the nose and tongue connected?
This picture shows what the inside of the nose and tongue look like from a side view. The back of the nose opens into the back of the throat.

👁 **FIND IT** INSIDE AND OUTSIDE
You'll need the magic lens to find some of these things.

1. nose
2. nostrils
3. smell detectors
4. olfactory bulb
5. mucus
6. tongue
7. taste buds
8. saliva

LOOK INSIDE

What happens up the nose and on the tongue?

The nose

1. The **nose** is mostly made from bendy cartilage, not from hard bone.

2. Two openings, called **nostrils,** open into the space inside the nose, which connects with the back of the mouth and tongue.

Mmm! When you smell food, your mouth makes watery saliva to help the food go down.

Smell

3. Breathe in and millions of **smell detectors** inside the nose pick up smells that stick to small finger-like endings.

4. The smell detectors send signals to the **olfactory bulb**, which sends signals to the brain to help work out each smell.

Atchoo!

5 Hairs inside the nose stop dust from getting into the body. **Mucus**, or snot, keeps the inside wet and helps it to smell. It also catches dirt and germs. Sneezing blows the mucus, dirt and germs out of the nose.

The smell of cooking can make you hungry. Your brain sends messages to your digestive system to say, "Get ready, food is on the way!"

Tasting food

6 The **tongue** helps to taste food. It also works with the teeth to mush up food so it's ready to swallow. This is the start of the journey of digestion.

7 **Taste buds** are the many small bumps on the tongue.

8 When food mixes with **saliva**, the taste buds send signals to the brain about the taste of the food.

How many taste buds are on a tongue?

A child has up to 10,000 taste buds, while an adult has only 6,000. Here are the five different tastes that taste buds recognize.

Bitter
A bitter taste can warn the body that it's about to eat bad or poisonous food.

Salty
Salty food can help the body work properly, but too much salt is bad for body health.

Sour
Lemons taste sour. Scientists think humans are the only animals to enjoy sour food.

Sweet
Sugary food tastes sweet and can give the body quick energy.

Umami
This is a super-charged savory taste. Soy sauce and mushrooms both have an umami flavor.

17

TEETH

How many teeth do you have?

It all depends on how old you are. A young child has 20 baby teeth, but one by one these fall out. New teeth grow. Usually, an adult has 32 teeth.

Can you touch your teeth with your tongue? Try to feel the pointy, sharp tops at the front and the flat tops at the back. Each tooth is different—it's perfectly shaped to rip, tear, or squash your food.

What's a tooth made from?

The outside of a tooth is made from shiny enamel. This is the hardest substance in the body. The part of a tooth you can see is called the crown. Inside, there is a hard tissue, called dentin. The root is the part of the tooth inside the gum.

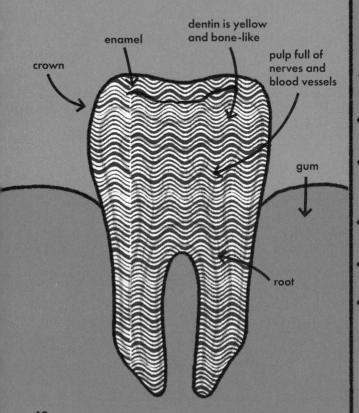

crown

enamel

dentin is yellow and bone-like

pulp full of nerves and blood vessels

gum

root

Why brush your teeth?

Brushing keeps your breath smelling sweet and prevents tooth decay. Brushing removes a sticky substance, called plaque. This is made by germs, called bacteria, that grow on leftover food in the mouth. The acid in the plaque eats into and decays your teeth. Brushing also helps to prevent gum disease. Try to remember to brush morning and night.

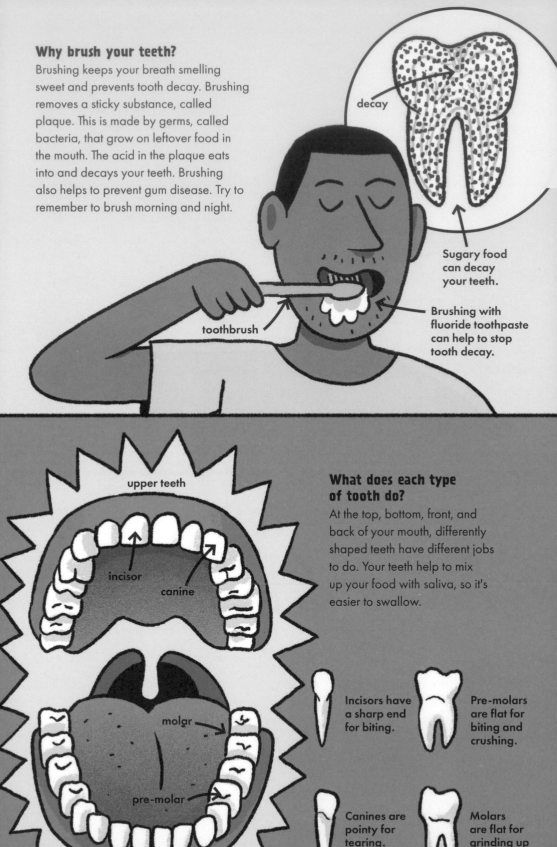

decay

Sugary food can decay your teeth.

Brushing with fluoride toothpaste can help to stop tooth decay.

toothbrush

upper teeth

incisor

canine

molar

pre-molar

lower teeth

What does each type of tooth do?

At the top, bottom, front, and back of your mouth, differently shaped teeth have different jobs to do. Your teeth help to mix up your food with saliva, so it's easier to swallow.

Incisors have a sharp end for biting.

Pre-molars are flat for biting and crushing.

Canines are pointy for tearing.

Molars are flat for grinding up food into little bits.

Braces help teeth to grow straight.

Why go for a dental check-up?

To keep your mouth and teeth healthy, especially when you're young. A dentist makes sure your teeth are growing properly. A check-up is also the time to look for decay before it spreads.

A dentist looks at the backs of teeth with a mirror.

What's a filling?

A dentist fills a hole made by decay with a filling. It stops the decay from spreading. In the picture, can you spot a filling made by the dentist?

What happens when you bite?

Crunch! Powerful muscles in your jaw work together. First, the lower jaw bites, then muscles move the jaw up and down and from side to side. The back molar teeth grind the fruit into mush. You're chewing, then—gulp—you swallow.

LOOK INSIDE

Find out what happens inside the mouth and how the teeth work.

1 lower jaw
2 upper jaw
3 muscles open and close the jaw

SKIN AND HAIR

How hairy is a human's body?

Hairy! A grown-up's body can have up to 5 million hairs from top to toe. That's as hairy as an ape, but human hairs are shorter, thinner, and harder to spot.

The human body is covered in hair, skin, and nails. The skin is a waterproof wrapping for the body. It helps to keep the insides of the body in and bad things, such as germs, out.

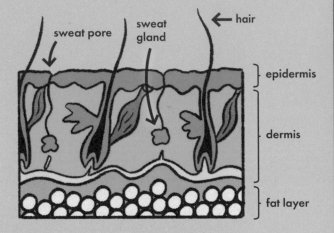

sweat pore · sweat gland · ← hair

epidermis

dermis

fat layer

What happens under the skin?

This picture shows up close the three layers of skin, called the epidermis, dermis, and fat layer.

👁 FIND IT INSIDE AND OUTSIDE

You'll need the magic lens to find some of these things.

❶ epidermis	❻ sweat gland
❷ dermis	❼ pore
❸ fat layer	❽ fingertips
❹ hair follicle	❾ nerves
❺ hair root	❿ nail plates

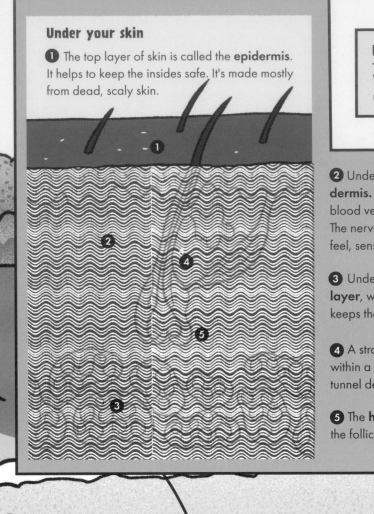

Under your skin

❶ The top layer of skin is called the **epidermis**. It helps to keep the insides safe. It's made mostly from dead, scaly skin.

LOOK INSIDE

What happens under the skin?

❷ Underneath the epidermis is the **dermis.** This thick layer is full of blood vessels and nerve endings. The nerve endings help the body to feel, sensing heat, cold, and pain.

❸ Underneath the dermis is a **fat layer**, which stores energy and keeps the body warm.

❹ A strand of bendy hair grows within a **hair follicle**, which is a tiny tunnel deep inside the skin.

❺ The **hair root** is at the base of the follicle.

Stay cool

❻ Sweat helps to keep the body cool. As it dries, it cools the body down. A **sweat gland** oozes sweat.

❼ The sweat comes out of a small opening, called a **pore**.

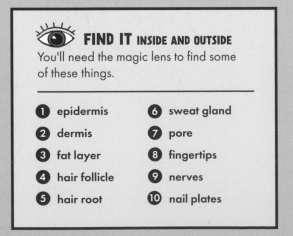

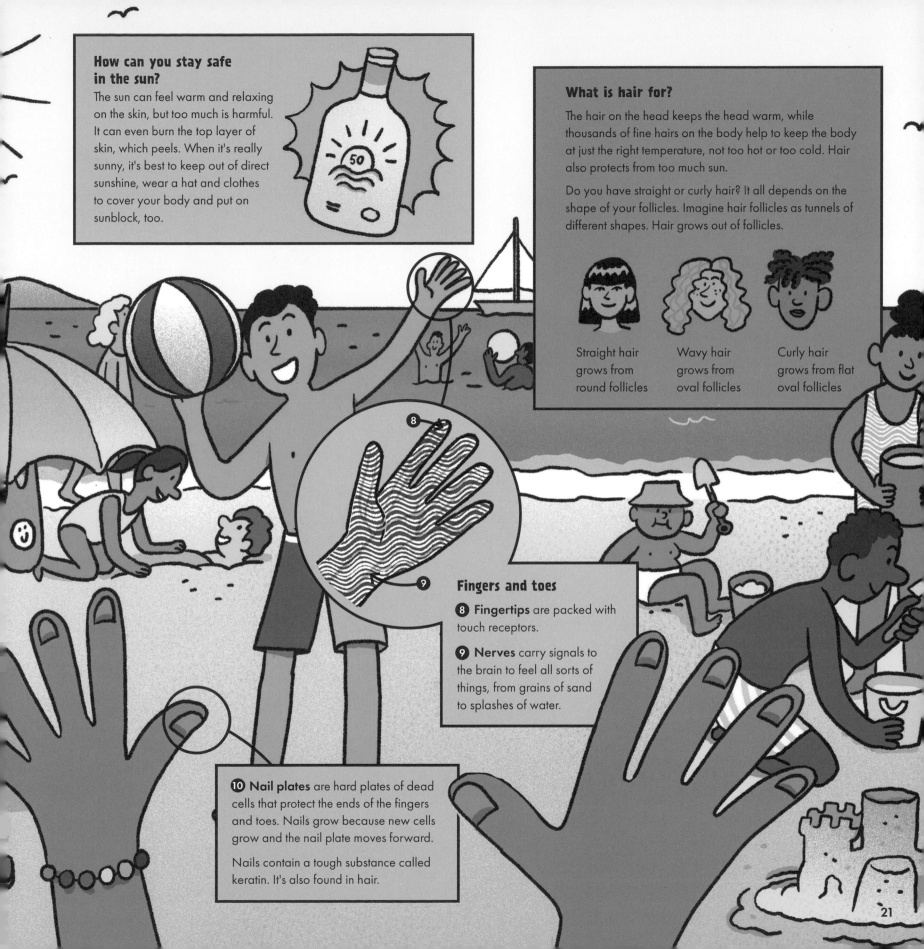

How can you stay safe in the sun?

The sun can feel warm and relaxing on the skin, but too much is harmful. It can even burn the top layer of skin, which peels. When it's really sunny, it's best to keep out of direct sunshine, wear a hat and clothes to cover your body and put on sunblock, too.

What is hair for?

The hair on the head keeps the head warm, while thousands of fine hairs on the body help to keep the body at just the right temperature, not too hot or too cold. Hair also protects from too much sun.

Do you have straight or curly hair? It all depends on the shape of your follicles. Imagine hair follicles as tunnels of different shapes. Hair grows out of follicles.

Straight hair grows from round follicles

Wavy hair grows from oval follicles

Curly hair grows from flat oval follicles

Fingers and toes

8 Fingertips are packed with touch receptors.

9 Nerves carry signals to the brain to feel all sorts of things, from grains of sand to splashes of water.

10 Nail plates are hard plates of dead cells that protect the ends of the fingers and toes. Nails grow because new cells grow and the nail plate moves forward.

Nails contain a tough substance called keratin. It's also found in hair.

BONES

Imagine if you didn't have bones inside your body.

You would be a blob! Over 200 bones of many shapes and sizes make the body's framework, called the skeleton. Can you feel some of your bones under your skin?

Hard bones keep the soft insides of the body safe, including the brain and heart. Meanwhile, stretchy muscles pull on bones to move the body, from hands that wave and hold a pencil to legs that run and jump.

What's inside a bone?

bone marrow

spongy bone

compact bone

Bones are strong and surprisingly light. The outside of a bone is hard and compact. Inside that is spongy bone that looks like honeycomb. In the middle there is a jelly, called bone marrow, which helps to make new blood cells.

👁 FIND IT INSIDE AND OUTSIDE

You'll need the magic lens to find some of these things.

1 skeleton
2 skull
3 joint
4 shoulder
5 ribs
6 elbow
7 spine
8 hip
9 knee
10 ankle

---

1 **Skeleton**

2 The **skull** is made from bones that fit together like a jigsaw. The skull protects the fragile brain.

3 A **joint** in the body is where two bones meet.

4 The **shoulder** is a ball-and-socket joint.

5 Curved bones, called **ribs**, make a cage to protect the delicate heart and lungs.

6 The **elbow** is a hinge joint.

7 The **spine** is the body's main support.

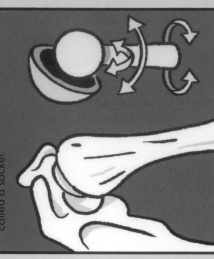

What's a ball-and-socket joint?

It's a type of joint that allows movement in many directions. If you can, try moving your arm and touching your shoulder. Now imagine a ball-shaped bone fitting into a cup-shaped bone, called a socket.

22

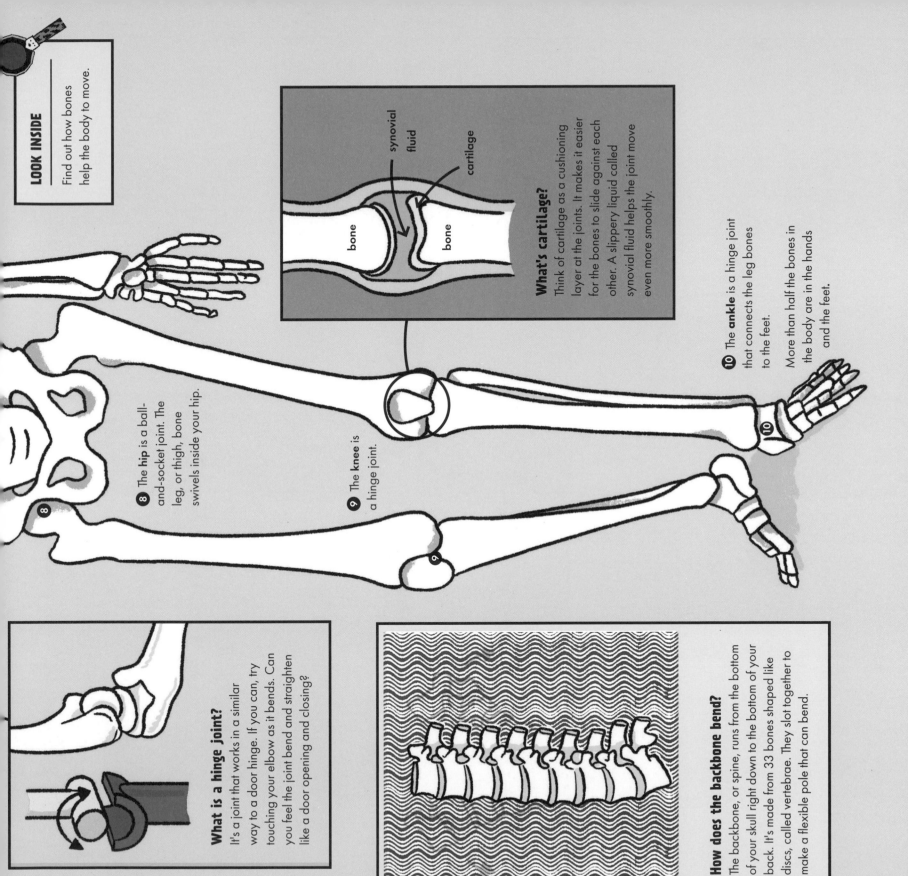

What's cartilage?

Think of cartilage as a cushioning layer at the joints. It makes it easier for the bones to slide against each other. A slippery liquid called synovial fluid helps the joint move even more smoothly.

synovial fluid

cartilage

bone

bone

8 The **hip** is a ball-and-socket joint. The leg, or thigh, bone swivels inside your hip.

9 The **knee** is a hinge joint.

10 The **ankle** is a hinge joint that connects the leg bones to the feet.

More than half the bones in the body are in the hands and the feet.

What is a hinge joint?

It's a joint that works in a similar way to a door hinge. If you can, try touching your elbow as it bends. Can you feel the joint bend and straighten like a door opening and closing?

How does the backbone bend?

The backbone, or spine, runs from the bottom of your skull right down to the bottom of your back. It's made from 33 bones shaped like discs, called vertebrae. They slot together to make a flexible pole that can bend.

23

MUSCLES

What happens inside the arm when it lifts at the elbow? Up, two, three, four!

A pair of muscles called the biceps and triceps works together pulling on the arm bones, and up the arm lifts.

Often muscles work in pairs. It's teamwork. Across the skeleton, more than 600 stretchy muscles pull on the bones to help move the body in all kinds of bendy ways.

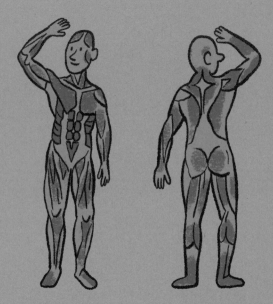

Where are there muscles in the body? There are muscles all over the body. This picture shows the muscles from top to toe.

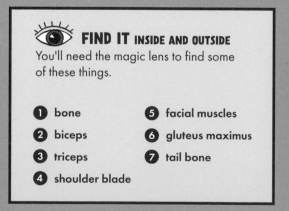

👁 **FIND IT** INSIDE AND OUTSIDE
You'll need the magic lens to find some of these things.

❶ bone   ❺ facial muscles

❷ biceps   ❻ gluteus maximus

❸ triceps   ❼ tail bone

❹ shoulder blade

Muscles push and pull

❶ To move a **bone**, muscles work in pairs doing the opposite of each other. One muscle contracts, or pulls, and the other relaxes. This is because a muscle can only pull on a bone and become shorter. It can't push.

When the arm lifts, two things happen:

❷ The **biceps** muscle contracts and becomes wider and shorter.

❸ And the **triceps** relaxes and becomes thinner and longer.

Together, the two muscles pull up the lower part of the arm.

❹ The **shoulder blade** helps keep the biceps and triceps muscles fixed in place.

And relax...

When the arm is straightened, the opposite happens.

❸ The **triceps** muscle contracts, or becomes shorter.

❷ Meanwhile, the **biceps** muscle relaxes. The triceps pulls down the lower part of the arm. The arm straightens.

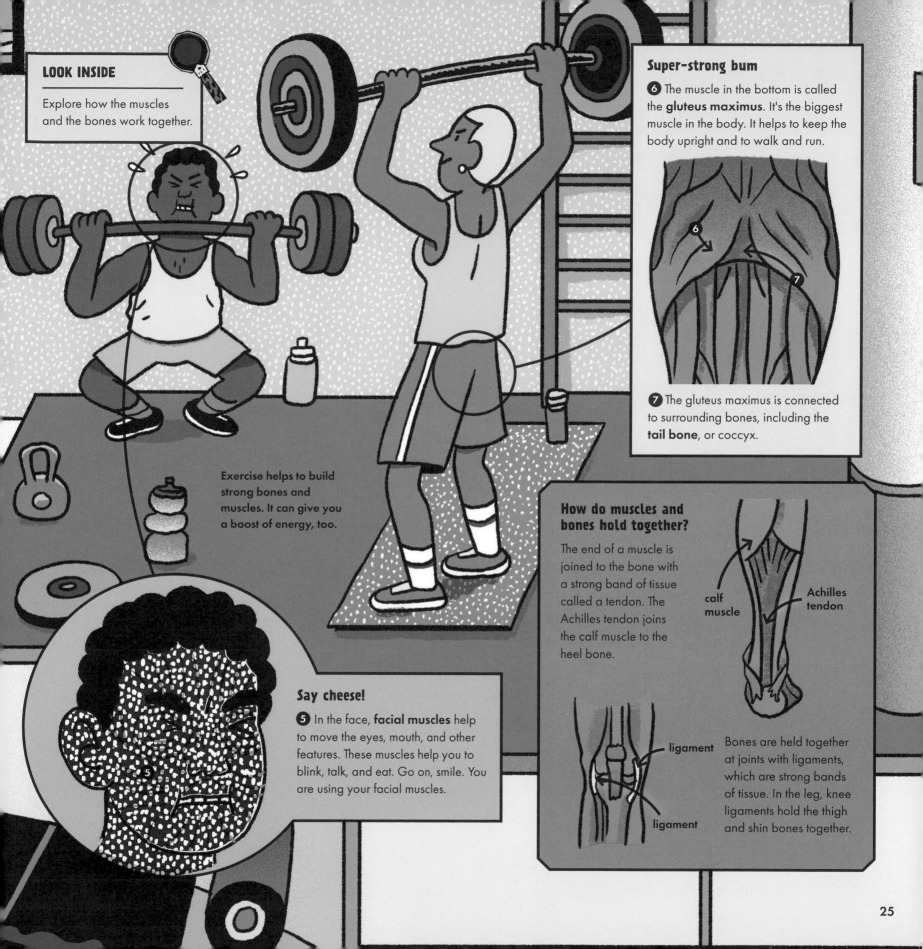

Exercise helps to build strong bones and muscles. It can give you a boost of energy, too.

Super-strong bum

6 The muscle in the bottom is called the **gluteus maximus**. It's the biggest muscle in the body. It helps to keep the body upright and to walk and run.

6

7

7 The gluteus maximus is connected to surrounding bones, including the **tail bone**, or coccyx.

How do muscles and bones hold together?

The end of a muscle is joined to the bone with a strong band of tissue called a tendon. The Achilles tendon joins the calf muscle to the heel bone.

calf muscle

Achilles tendon

ligament

ligament

Bones are held together at joints with ligaments, which are strong bands of tissue. In the leg, knee ligaments hold the thigh and shin bones together.

Say cheese!

5 In the face, **facial muscles** help to move the eyes, mouth, and other features. These muscles help you to blink, talk, and eat. Go on, smile. You are using your facial muscles.

5

LUNGS

Why does exercise make us huff and puff?

During exercise, we breathe faster and take in more oxygen from the air so the muscles can work harder than usual. Phew!

Your lungs are in your chest. You breathe air in and out of your lungs through your nose and mouth. The lungs take oxygen from the air into the body to keep it working.

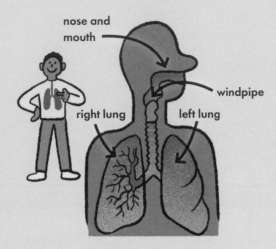

nose and mouth

windpipe

right lung

left lung

How does air move into the lungs?
This picture shows how air moves through the mouth and nose, then down the windpipe to the lungs.

 FIND IT INSIDE AND OUTSIDE
You'll need the magic lens to find some of these things.

1	windpipe	**5**	diaphragm
2	voice box	**6**	bronchi
3	lungs	**7**	bronchioles
4	ribcage	**8**	alveoli

LOOK INSIDE

Find out what happens inside your body when you breathe in and out.

What happens when you breathe in?

Try putting your hands on your ribs and breathing in. Can you feel your ribs pulling upward and outward? This helps to make more room inside your chest.

1 Air from the nose and mouth travels down the **windpipe** into the lungs. The lining of the windpipe is covered with tiny hair-like structures, which catch dirt and germs.

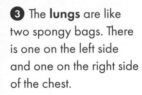

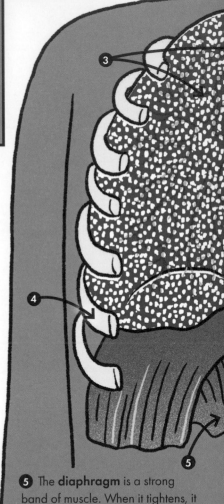

3 The **lungs** are like two spongy bags. There is one on the left side and one on the right side of the chest.

The left lung makes room for the heart.

Mucus in the lungs picks up germs. You cough up the mucus to get rid of the germs.

4 The bones of the **ribcage** protect the lungs and heart.

5 The **diaphragm** is a strong band of muscle. When it tightens, it becomes flatter, making more space inside your chest. Air rushes into your lungs and you are breathing in. When the diaphragm relaxes again, air is pushed out of your lungs and you are breathing out.

2 The **voice box** is part of the windpipe. Air rushes between a small gap made by the vocal cords, then sounds come out. When you speak, some sounds are made in your voice box.

What happens when you breathe out?

Now try putting your hands on your ribcage and breathing out. Can you feel your ribs falling back down? There's less room now inside your chest, so the used-up air gets pushed out, making room for fresh air the next time you breathe in.

What is asthma?

It's a medical condition that makes it difficult to breathe. It happens when the tubes inside the lungs become narrow or swollen. An inhaler can help to open up the tubes so air flows more easily to the lungs. Allergies can make asthma worse.

Inside the lungs

6 Inside each lung air travels through big tubes, called **bronchi**, that branch into smaller and smaller tubes. The tubes look like upside-down trees.

What are hiccups?

Hiccups happen when the diaphragm suddenly tightens, pulling in air. Then—"hic"—the vocal cords snap closed. Hiccups can start for lots of reasons, including eating a large meal or drinking a carbonated drink.

Hic!

7 The smallest tubes are called **bronchioles**.

8 At the end of each bronchiole there are tiny sacs, called **alveoli**, in bunches like grapes. Oxygen seeps through the bubbly walls into the blood.

The lungs and heart work together to move oxygen from the air into the blood and to all parts of the body.

HEART

What does the heart do non-stop?

It pumps blood all the way around the body—in about 60 seconds. Think of your heart as a pumping engine that never stops.

About 70 times a minute, the heart pumps blood that is full of oxygen and goodness from the food you eat to every part of the body. The heart is a vital organ and keeps you alive.

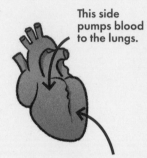

This side pumps blood to the lungs.

This side pumps blood to the body.

Where is your heart?

Your heart is in your chest. This picture shows that your heart has two sides that pump blood around the body.

👁 FIND IT INSIDE AND OUTSIDE

You'll need the magic lens to find some of these things.

1 plasma	**6** lungs
2 red blood cells	**7** valves
3 platelets	**8** capillary
4 white blood cells	**9** artery
5 heart	**10** vein

What's in your blood?

1 Blood is made from a fluid called **plasma**, which is mostly water, plus three types of blood cells, called red blood cells, platelets, and white blood cells.

2 Nearly half of blood is made from **red blood cells**. These cells take oxygen to other cells and remove carbon dioxide from them.

This picture shows the blood cells much bigger than they really are, as if through a microscope.

4 **White blood cells** help fight infection. They hunt down and kill germs.

3 **Platelets** help blood to clot, or thicken, and make a scab on a wound.

LOOK INSIDE

Discover what happens when your heart beats.

Exercise can help to strengthen your heart and keep it in the best condition possible.

How does the heart pump blood around the body?

5 The **heart** works like a machine with two connected sides that pump. One side pumps blood to the lungs to receive oxygen. The other side pumps blood full of oxygen to the rest of the body.

6 The **lungs** and the heart work together to keep the blood full of oxygen.

7 Each side of the heart has **valves** that open and close to control the flow of blood.

How does blood flow?

Blood flows from the heart through blood vessels, which are similar to roads around the body that loop back to the heart. There are three types of blood vessels.

8 A **capillary** is the smallest blood vessel. Oxygen seeps through its thin walls.

9 An **artery** is a thick tube that carries blood away from the heart.

10 A **vein** is a thin tube that carries blood back to the heart.

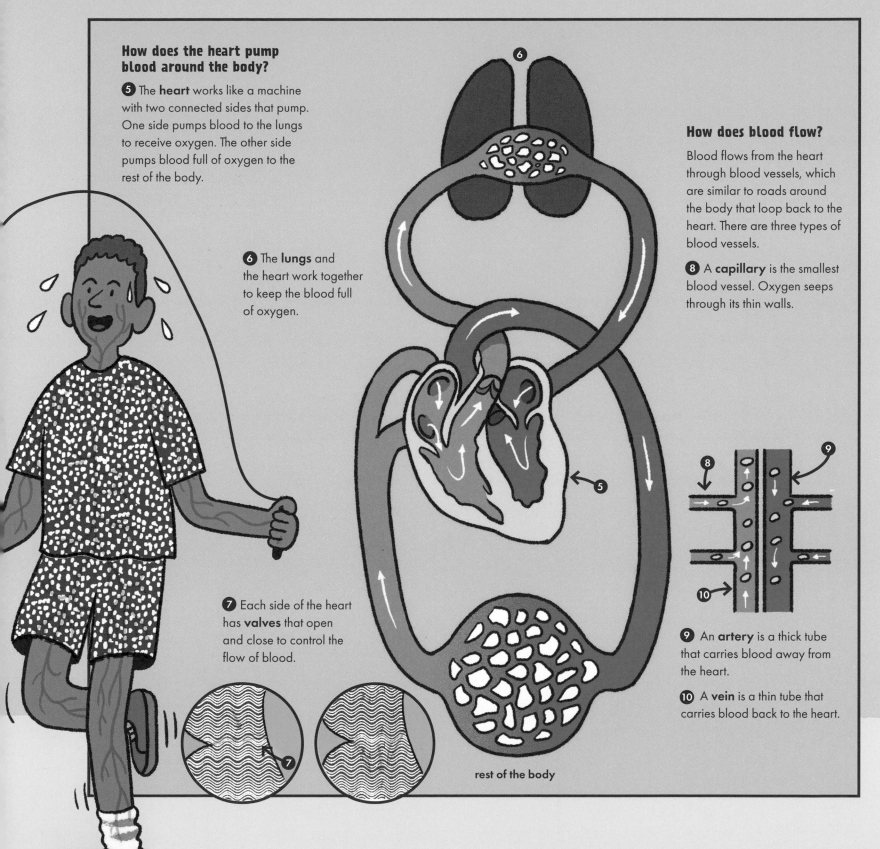

rest of the body

EATING AND DRINKING

Excuse me! What's happening when your stomach gurgles and growls?

It's the sound of bubbles of air mixed with food and juices from your insides. Your dinner is on the move through your body.

Down the food goes through one long tube from your mouth to your bottom. Along the way, the good bits, called nutrients, are absorbed by the body. This journey of food is called digestion.

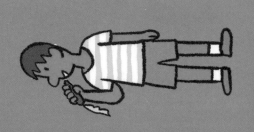

👁 FIND IT INSIDE AND OUTSIDE

You'll need the magic lens to find some of these things.

- ① teeth
- ② tongue
- ③ epiglottis
- ④ esophagus
- ⑤ trachea
- ⑥ stomach
- ⑦ liver
- ⑧ gall bladder
- ⑨ small intestine
- ⑩ villi
- ⑪ large intestine
- ⑫ poop
- ⑬ kidneys
- ⑭ bladder

LOOK INSIDE

Discover how food is digested in the body. It's a team effort of body parts.

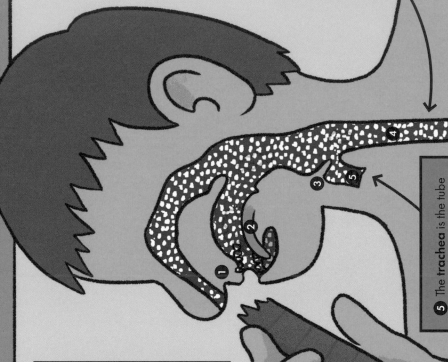

muscles push the food down

④ The food travels down a food pipe, called the **esophagus**. Muscles push the food down into the stomach.

⑤ The **trachea** is the tube you breathe through. If, by mistake, the food gets in it, you cough to push it up.

① First, **teeth** grind the food and mix it with saliva. Special proteins, called enzymes, help to break down the food.

② The **tongue** moves the food around the mouth and helps to push it down the throat. It's time to swallow.

③ A flap, called the **epiglottis**, stops the food from going down the wrong way.

6 Inside the **stomach**, muscles churn up the food into mush. The stomach is full of strong acidic juices that help to break down the food.

When your stomach is empty, it sends a message to the brain and you feel HUNGRY. It's time to eat again.

10 The lining of the small intestine is covered in tiny finger-type bumps, called **villi**. They help to absorb nutrients.

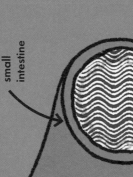

small intestine

villi

It takes about one day for food to pass through your body, from eating to going to the bathroom.

11 Once the food has been digested, or broken down, watery waste collects in the **large intestine**. Lots of the water is sucked back into the bloodstream.

12 Finally, the waste is pushed out of your body as **poop**.

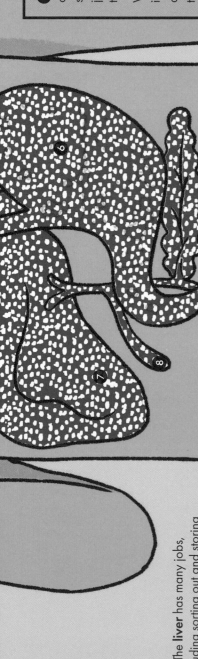

7 The **liver** has many jobs, including sorting out and storing nutrients. It makes a thick yellow juice, called bile, that helps to break down fatty food.

8 Bile from the liver is stored in the **gall bladder** until it is needed.

9 In the **small intestine**, the nutrients are absorbed. They soak through the lining into the blood, which carries the food's goodness around the body.

What is pee?

Pee is waste water from the body.

13 The **kidneys** control the amount of water in the body. They wash away any waste and spare water.

This water is turned into pee. It drips down two tubes, called ureters.

14 All the pee collects in a stretchy bag, called the **bladder**. When the bladder is full, you feel the urge and off you go to the bathroom.

All the cells in the body need water to work properly.

STAYING HEALTHY

How does your body keep you healthy and fight off sickness?

Many parts of the body work together to keep you well. Together, your body's protection unit is called the immune system.

Protection starts on the outside. Your skin stops germs invading your body. Saliva kills germs in your mouth. And sticky mucus up your nose traps germs, too.

LOOK INSIDE

Discover how the body fights off sickness.

How do germs make you sick?

All kinds of germ invaders try to attack the body, including bacteria and viruses. If these germs get inside the body, they can spread as an **infection** and make you feel ill.

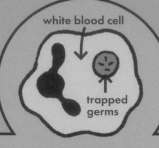

white blood cell

trapped germs

How does the body fight an infection?

It's time to attack! The body's white blood cells make weapons called **antibodies**. These stick to germs and tell white blood cells that the germs are the enemy. At the same time, other white blood cells hunt out germs to destroy. They circle then trap and digest the germs.

Some people have weakened immune systems. Doctors provide special medicines to give them a boost.

What's a virus?

It's a tiny structure that can cause disease. First, the virus invades one cell. Then this cell becomes a virus factory, making new copies of the virus. These infect more and more cells so the virus spreads.

virus invades cell and multiplies

VIRUS PREVENTION

What's a vaccine?

A vaccine protects the body from catching an infectious disease. Usually, a vaccine is an injection. A vaccine teaches the immune system how to fight off the disease. Some vaccines can protect you from the disease for many years.

Ouch! A deep cut to the skin is called a wound. Slowly over time, new skin grows back, until the wound heals.

How does a cut heal?

When the skin is broken, the body goes into action quickly.

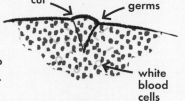

cut germs
white blood cells

1 White blood cells speed to the cut and kill any germs.

2 Near the cut, platelets thicken the blood so it can form a scab, which will stop more germs from getting in.

Sometimes, a green-yellow pus forms. This is mostly dead white blood cells that killed the germs.

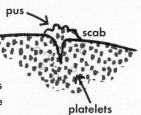

pus
scab
platelets

3 Over time, the skin heals. Soon the scab falls off to show new skin underneath.

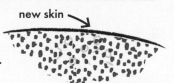

new skin

What is an allergy?

It's when your body reacts to certain substances as though they are harmful. You might start sneezing because of dust or pollen in the air or animals at home. Some allergies can be more dangerous and cause breathing or heart problems.

What are bacteria?

They are tiny living things. Each bacterium is made of just one cell. Many are harmless and some even help us. But when harmful bacteria get into the body, they cause infections and illness.

antibiotic

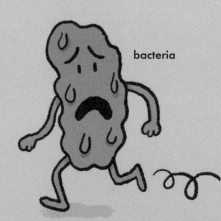

bacteria

What medicine stops an infection?

Antibiotics help to fight infections caused by bacteria. Antibiotics can work like a team of powerful boxers that attack the walls of bacteria. Antibiotics may kill bacteria or stop them from multiplying. They can also kill good bacteria, so they should be used only when needed.

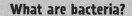

33

OFF TO THE DOCTOR'S

What happens at the doctor's office?

The medical team works like detectives searching for clues about why you might feel unwell. The doctor or nurse asks questions about how you feel inside and out.

Often, signs on the outside of the body help to show what's happening on the inside. Do you feel hotter than usual? Do you have a rash? A look into the ears and mouth can show how the body is working, too.

What's happening inside?
The doctor might listen to the inside of your chest through a stethoscope. By listening to your heartbeat or breathing, the doctor can hear if there are problems with the heart or lungs.

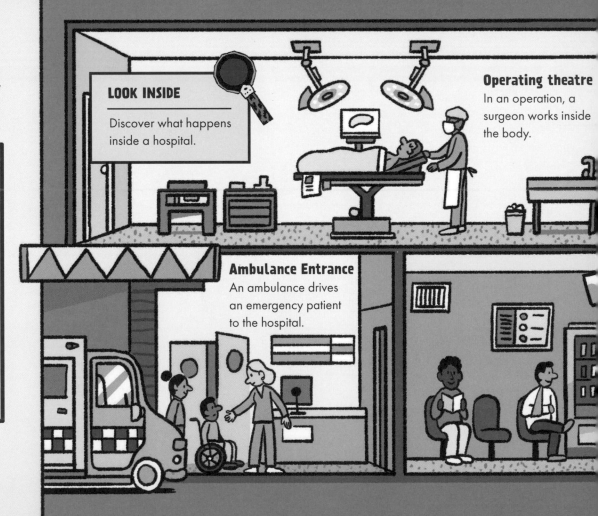

What happens at a hospital?
At a hospital, specialist doctors, nurses, and all kinds of health workers care for patients. In an emergency, a patient sees a doctor immediately in the Emergency Room. An inpatient is a patient who sleeps overnight at the hospital.

LOOK INSIDE

Discover what happens inside a hospital.

Operating theatre
In an operation, a surgeon works inside the body.

Ambulance Entrance
An ambulance drives an emergency patient to the hospital.

OUTPATIENT DEPARTMENTS

 Opthalmology – eyes

 Ears, nose, and throat

 Dermatology – skin

 Radiology – X-rays and scans

 Orthopedics – bones and muscles

 Respiratory – lungs

 Cardiology – heart

 Maternity – giving birth

 Pathology – blood and tissue tests

An outpatient visits the hospital for an appointment at one of the many specialist departments.

What is a thermometer?

A thermometer shows the temperature, or warmth, of your body as a measurement. If your temperature is higher than normal, it might mean that there are germs inside your body.

What are symptoms?

Symptoms are ways that you or your body feel out of the ordinary. You just don't feel your usual self.

What's a diagnosis?

A diagnosis could be the name of the illness that might be causing your symptoms. Or it could be the name just for the way that you are because everyone is different. Once you have a diagnosis, the doctor might prescribe medicine or send you to a specialist at the hospital.

...ray department

...X-ray is a test that ...ws pictures of inside ...body, especially ...ken bones.

The x-ray technician stands behind a screen.

Blood tests

A small amount of blood is taken then tested in a laboratory.

On the floor

An inpatient might be cared for by nurses and doctors in a hospital room.

Emergency Room

First, a doctor examines the patient, then decides what tests are needed and if the patient should see a specialist.

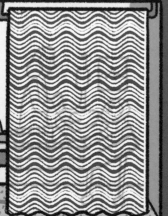

Scanner

A scanner is a machine that shows pictures of many organs inside the body.

A doctor studies the pictures to help decide how to treat the patient.

35

IN SURGERY

What's an operation?

It's when a doctor, called a surgeon, cuts open and works inside the body to help improve the health of the patient.

First, a team of expert doctors and nurses scrub in, which means they thoroughly wash their hands and arms to stop any germs, then put on protective gear.

👁 FIND IT INSIDE AND OUTSIDE

You'll need the magic lens to find some of these things.

1. operating room
2. lights
3. anesthesiologist
4. surgeon
5. masks, gowns, and gloves
6. scalpel
7. clamps
8. retractor
9. blood and fluids
10. stitches

What's keyhole surgery?

It's when a surgeon makes a tiny snip into a patient, almost like a keyhole. The surgeon feeds in a tube with a camera and a light on the end. Then a computer shows real-time video of the inside of the body. The surgeon inserts special tools into the hole and repairs the body, watching what they're doing on the video.

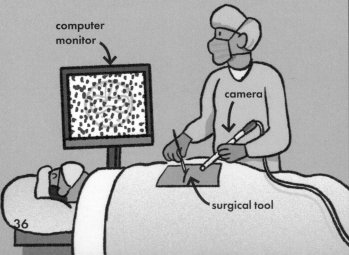

computer monitor

camera

surgical tool

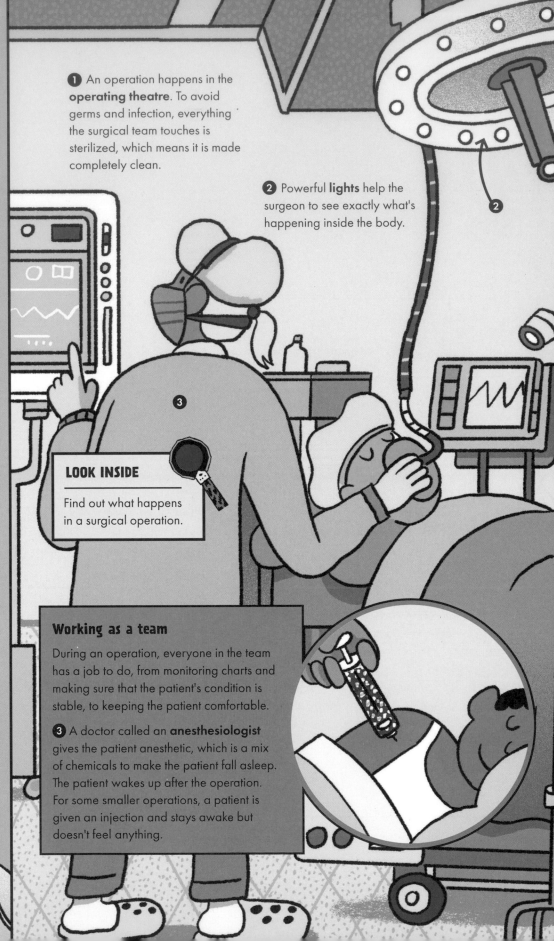

❶ An operation happens in the **operating theatre**. To avoid germs and infection, everything the surgical team touches is sterilized, which means it is made completely clean.

❷ Powerful **lights** help the surgeon to see exactly what's happening inside the body.

LOOK INSIDE

Find out what happens in a surgical operation.

Working as a team

During an operation, everyone in the team has a job to do, from monitoring charts and making sure that the patient's condition is stable, to keeping the patient comfortable.

❸ A doctor called an **anesthesiologist** gives the patient anesthetic, which is a mix of chemicals to make the patient fall asleep. The patient wakes up after the operation. For some smaller operations, a patient is given an injection and stays awake but doesn't feel anything.

4 The **surgeon** is trained to cut open and work inside the body.

5 The team wears **masks, gowns, and gloves** to stop infections from spreading.

Who works in surgery?

As well as the surgeon and anesthesiologist, nurses train to work in an operating room. Support workers make the process run smoothly. And medical staff prepare patients for their operations then look after them in recovery.

Making the cut

The surgeon uses surgical instruments, or tools.

6 A **scalpel** cuts into the flesh.

7 **Clamps** hold flesh and organs in place.

8 A **retractor** holds the flesh out of the way.

9 During the operation, **blood and fluids** might be given to the patient through a tube into a blood vessel.

10 At the end of the operation, the surgeon closes the wound with **stitches**, staples, or special glue. Staples and some stitches need to be taken out a few weeks later.

What happens after surgery?

A team of nurses looks after the patient until they are well enough to go home. This might be later that day, the next morning or in a few days.

At home, the patient must follow the advice given at the hospital. It's important to rest and build up strength.

HEALTHY AND HAPPY

What does your body need inside and out?

It needs lots of things: healthy food for tons of energy, regular washing to keep clean, exercise to stay fit, loads of fresh air, and plenty of sleep at night.

Try to remember to check in with your emotions and think about how you feel on the inside, too. What goes on inside your mind is called your mental health.

How can you eat healthily every day?

– It's fun to experiment with new delicious tastes. Try to eat a variety of foods.

– At mealtimes, try to eat a healthy, balanced plate of food, including protein, carbohydrates, such as whole-grain bread or brown rice to keep you full, plus plenty of vegetables.

– Snacks, such as sweets and chips, are high in sugar, fat, and salt. Try to keep these foods just for special treats.

Protein such as eggs, beans, meat, and fish helps muscles, bones, skin, and many organs work.

Fats give you energy but you don't need much. Try to eat more fats from plants and fish than from other animals.

Why do you need to sleep?

Sleep recharges the body's batteries so that you are full of energy for the next day. Overnight, cells in the body repair and new cells grow. The brain works in a different way from when you're awake so that it can work at full speed the next day.

During sleep, you dream. Your brain sorts information from the day to help make memories.

Don't forget to wash your hands!

Think of all the things you touch every day, from a pet to your runny nose! A good way to stop germs in their tracks is to keep clean. Try to remember to wash your hands often, especially after going to the bathroom and before eating.

Wash with soap and warm water.

Keep your hands under the tap and count up to 15.

Don't forget to wash your nails and knuckles.

Calcium in milk and leafy vegetables helps build strong bones and teeth.

Rainbow-colored fruit and vegetables are high in fiber and keep your gut healthy. Try to eat five portions a day.

And don't forget...
Drink plenty of water—up to eight glasses every day.

Carbohydrates in bread and potatoes give you short bursts of energy.

Take care of your mental health
If you are worried about something, try speaking with an adult you trust. Chatting with friends and playing in nature can help to take your mind off things, too. When mental health concerns are serious, you can talk to a mental health specialist.

How does exercise help the body?
Exercise helps bones and muscles to stay strong. It also releases endorphins, which are chemicals that put you in a good mood. Even a little bit of exercise can make you feel on top of the world. Try exercising by yourself or with friends. Get your family involved, too, if you can.

It's fun finding the exercise you enjoy most. It could be trampolining...

...going for a walk...

...skipping rope...

...playing sports...

...riding a bike, or something else!

BABIES AND GROWING UP

How fast does a newborn baby grow?

Fast. In the first year, a baby can triple in size. Usually, we humans keep growing until our teens, but more slowly—or we'd be giants.

A baby grows into a child, then a teenager, then an adult. This adult might make a new baby, who grows up. Then this grown-up might make another baby. And on the circle goes.

Who's in your family?

Families come in all shapes and sizes, but generations work in the same way. Your grandparents are the parents of your parents.

👁 FIND IT INSIDE AND OUTSIDE
You'll need the magic lens to find some of these things.

1. twins
2. newborn baby
3. toddler
4. child
5. teenager
6. adult

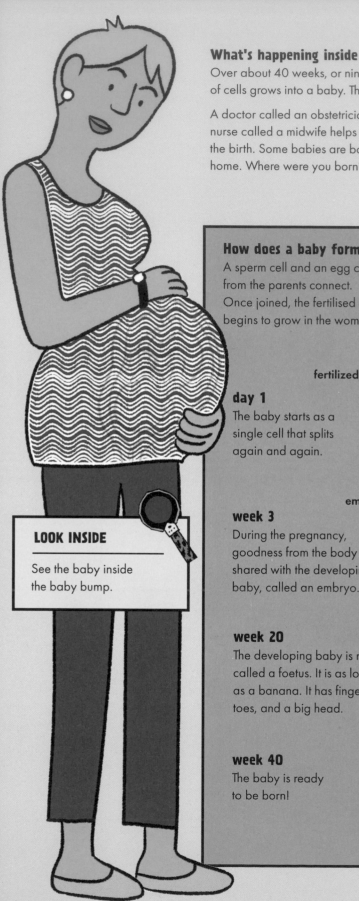

What's happening inside a "baby bump?"

Over about 40 weeks, or nine months, a tiny collection of cells grows into a baby. This time is called pregnancy.

A doctor called an obstetrician or a specially trained nurse called a midwife helps during pregnancy and at the birth. Some babies are born in a hospital, others at home. Where were you born?

LOOK INSIDE

See the baby inside the baby bump.

How does a baby form?

A sperm cell and an egg cell from the parents connect. Once joined, the fertilised egg begins to grow in the womb.

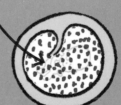
sperm   egg

fertilized egg

day 1
The baby starts as a single cell that splits again and again.

embryo

week 3
During the pregnancy, goodness from the body is shared with the developing baby, called an embryo.

week 20
The developing baby is now called a foetus. It is as long as a banana. It has fingers, toes, and a big head.

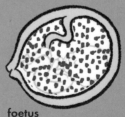
foetus

week 40
The baby is ready to be born!

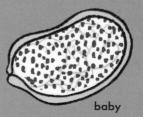
baby

Growing up

From the moment you are born, your body changes. First, you grow up. Usually, at about the age of 20, you stop growing in height. In old age, the body can slow down.

2 A **newborn baby** needs to be fed and kept safe and warm. Slowly, a baby learns to crawl, then stand.

3 A **toddler** explores the world, walking, talking, and asking questions. The toddler's brain learns many new things quickly.

4 A **child** still grows but more slowly. The body and the brain can learn all kinds of new things, such as how to ride a bike or new skills at school. It's a time for playing and learning.

1 **Twins** grow together inside a baby bump.

5 Over many years, a **teenager** grows to look more like an adult. In this time of change, a teenager might sleep more, have pimples, and feel moody.

6 When you are an **adult**, your body still changes but more slowly. Grown-ups might make new babies.

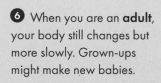

What is puberty?
It's a time when a child grows into an adult.

Special messengers, called hormones, set off different stages of life, from birth to old age. A teenager has particular hormones that tell different parts of the body to change. Some make the body have growth spurts. Others help the body to change in ways that mean that it can make children.

41

IN THE LAB

What medicines are doctors inventing right now?

In the laboratory, scientists are carrying out all kinds of exciting research into how the body works and how to keep it healthy.

The scientists combine a detailed understanding of how the body works with new technologies. They design clever medical treatments, machines, and tests.

What's a nanobot?

It's a minuscule robot. A nanobot is so small ten could sit on the width of a human hair. In the future, a nanobot might be injected into the blood to perform medical operations. It could kill germs, repair damaged cells, and deliver medicine to exactly the right spot in the body.

Can body parts be printed out?

In the future, maybe. Scientists are carrying out amazing research into printing body parts on a 3D printer. This is called bioprinting. The body part could be for a patient who needs an organ replaced. Layers of human cells would be printed to form a body part, such as the kidneys.

What are bionics?

Bionics are artificial replacement parts of the body to help people who need them. A bionic leg can pick up signals from the muscles to move and bend, just like a real leg. Scientists are also working on a bionic eye that connects with the brain to help a person see.

LOOK INSIDE

Explore how scientists are inventing new ways of treating people.

A bionic eye may one day help blind people to see.

What are genes?

Your genes are the instructions that make you the only you in the world. Genes are made of DNA, which is found in structures called chromosomes in almost all your cells. Doctors can now test genes and DNA to help spot diseases, often before they develop. One day, a technology called gene editing might be able to cut away or replace genes that cause disease.

DNA   chromosome   cell

What's a stem cell?

Imagine a cell that has extra-special powers. Stem cells are the first cells that form to make a baby. They can be steered or turned into different kinds of body cells. In the future, it might be possible to put stem cells back into the body to repair other damaged cells. This could help to stop some diseases.

stem cell

nerve cell

blood cell

muscle cell

Is medicine smart?

Yes, and it's getting smarter. Everybody's body is slightly different—we are all unique. Scientists are researching medicines that are tailored to work for one particular patient at a time. This is called personalized medicine. It uses technology to discover a person's own unique make-up, based on their genes.

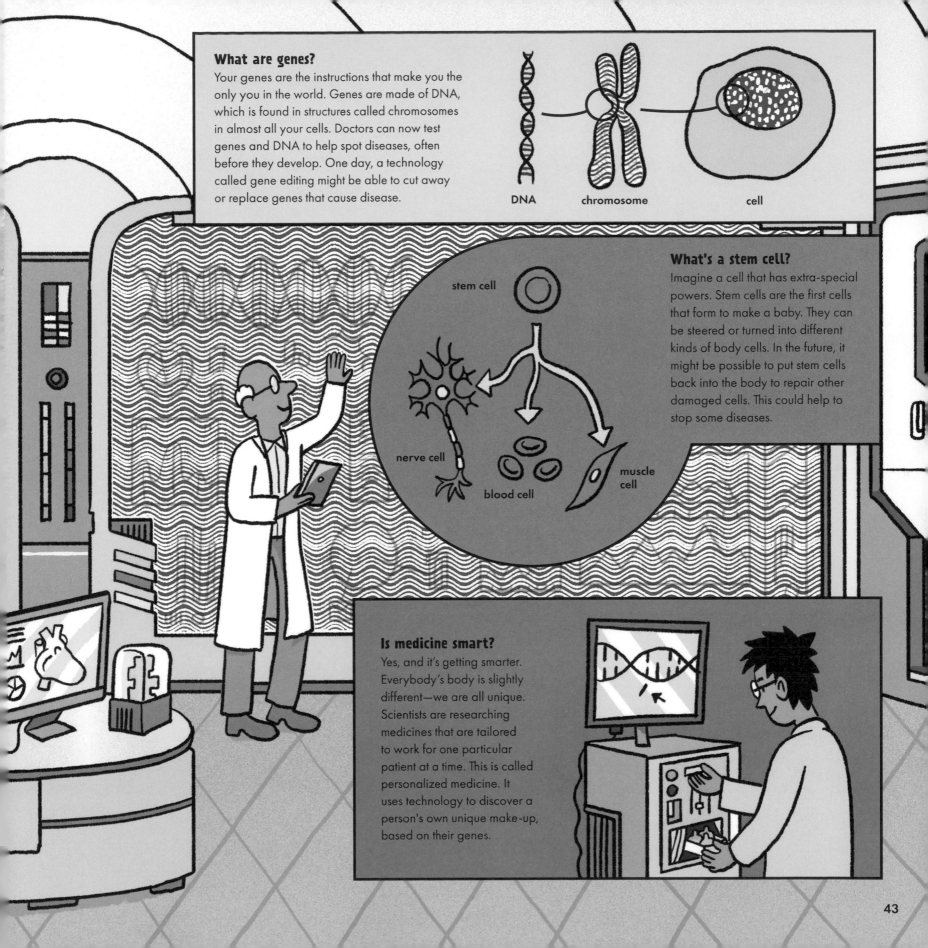

ALL TYPES OF BODIES

Bodies come in all shapes and sizes. Over time, a body changes, too. Your body might look different and work differently to somebody else's body.

Always remember to treat everybody with respect—don't ask questions about somebody else's body unless they tell you it's okay to do so. Everybody is different and everybody is special.

INDEX

SOURCE NOTES

This book was developed in collaboration with specialist medical consultants and reference material from books, videos and online articles. Below is a selection of resources to explore if you want to know more about some of the topics in this book.

– JW

"12 innovations that will revolutionise the future of medicine," National Geographic (www.nationalgeographic.co.uk)

"Adaptive immunity," Khan Academy (www.khanacademy.org)

"All About The Brain: Anatomy, Conditions, and Keeping It Healthy," Healthline (www.healthline.com)

"Anatomy of the Skin," Stanford Children's Health (www.stanfordchildrens.org)

"Brain areas and their functions," health24 (www.news24.com/health24)

"Do you know what happens to your sample?," Institute of Biomedical Science (www.ibms.org)

"How Cells Work," how stuff works (www.science.howstuffworks.com)

"How Human Memory Works," how stuff works (www.science.howstuffworks.com)

"How the ear works," Hearing Link (www.hearinglink.org)

"How the Lungs Work," National Heart, Lung, and Blood Institute (www.nhlbi.nih.gov)

"How your heart works," British Heart Foundation (www.bhf.org.uk)

"Human Body," Britannica (www.britannica.com)

"Human Body," DK findout! (www.dkfindout.com)

Knowledge Encyclopedia Human Body! (UK: Dorling Kindersley, 2017)

"KS2, Human Body," BBC Bitesize (www.bbc.co.uk/bitesize/topics/zcyycdm)

"Live Well," NHS (www.nhs.uk/live-well/)

"Lobes of the brain," The University of Queensland Australia (www.qbi.uq.edu.au)

Stowell, Louie. Look Inside Your Body (UK: Usborne, 2012)

www.neurotransmissions.science/videos/

"Parts of the brain and their functions," Read Biology (www.readbiology.com)

Walliman, Dr Dominic. Professor Astro Cat's Human Body Odyssey (UK: Flying Eye, 2018)

Daynes, Katie. See Inside Your Body (UK: Usborne, 2006)

"The A to Z of NHS hospital departments in the UK," netdoctor (www.netdoctor.co.uk)

"The Cerebellum Is Your "Little Brain"—and It Does Some Pretty Big Things," Scientific American (www.scientificamerican.com)

"The Circulatory System: An Amazing Circuit That Keeps Our Bodies Going," Live Science (www.livescience.com)

"The Eatwell Guide," NHS (www.nhs.uk)

"The Future of Medicine," Cambridge Universiry (www.youtube.com/watch?v=ZGGDKC3Glrl&ab_channel=CambridgeUniversity)

"The Human Skeletal System," Live Science (www.livescience.com)

"The Science of Taste," Food Insight (www.foodinsight.org)

"Theatre support worker," NHS (www.healthcareers.nhs.uk/explore-roles)

"Tooth Anatomy Education," VC Dental (www.vcdental.com.au)

"What's it like to work in an operating theatre?," Sheffield Hallam University (www.shu.ac.uk)

"Why vaccination is safe and important," NHS (www.nhs.uk)

"Your Eyes," Kids Health (kidshealth.org)